SABASTIAN VETTEL
GENIUS OR JOKER?

German formula 1 race driver retires, (insight story)

All rights reserved.
Copyright © July 2022 by
SILVERBRAIN PUBLICATIONS

TABLE OF CONTENT

INTRODUCTION
CHAPTER ONE
- BIOGRAPHY
- EARLY CHILDHOOD & LIFE
- CAREER STATS
- AWARDS & ACHIEVEMENTS
- PERSONAL LIFE

CHAPTER TWO
- REASONS FOR SABASTIAN RETIREMENT REVEILED

Chapter one

INTRODUCTION

BIOGRAPHY

German race-car driver Sebastian Vettel is presently competing in Formula 1 for Aston Martin. Previously, he raced for Red Bull, Toro Rosso, BMW, and Ferrari. He is one of just four drivers who have won four or more championships in Formula 1. He became the youngest race winner, the youngest to win the World Drivers' Championship, and the youngest double, treble, and quadruple world champion in Formula 1, because of his unrelenting passion for success. Dietrich Mateschitz, the owner of Red Bull, characterized him as a young man with exceptional promise. He is quick, smart, and highly interested in technology. Because of his driving style, focus, and role with his engineers behind the scenes, he is frequently likened to the late German racing driver Michael Schumacher. He collaborates closely with the designers because he is passionate about various helmet designs. He celebrated creating his 50th helmet design in 2012. He always gives his vehicles nick names since he thinks it's necessary to develop a deep bond with them. He believes it is seductive to name an automobile after a woman.

EARLY CHILDHOOD & LIFE

Norbert and Heike Vettel welcomed Sebastian into the world on July 3, 1987 in Heppenheim, Germany. He has a younger brother, Fabian, who is also a racing driver, as well as two elder sisters, Melanie and Stefanie.

At the age of 4, Sebastian Vettel began amateur karting, and at the age of 8, he started competing in kart series. He was accepted into the Red Bull Junior Team when he was eleven.

In 2001, he won the Junior Monaco Kart Cup, among other junior championships.

He succeeded in his Starkenburg Gymnasium graduation exams. Michael Schumacher, Michael Jackson, and Michael Jordan were his boyhood idols.

CAREER STATS

Sebastian Vettel advanced through the lesser levels of motorsport in an astoundingly short period of time and with great success. He won the Formula 1 world championship at the earliest age ever in 2010, and he has retained it ever since.

The German Junior Karting Championship, Monaco Kart Cup, and European Junior Karting Championship were among the titles Vettel won throughout his eight years of karting in 2001. He finished sixth in the Senior ICA Kart Championship the following year before switching to car racing.

He was the top rookie and placed second in the 2003 Formula BMW Germany championship. The following year, at the age of 17, he resoundingly captured the championship with 18 victories from 20 races and 387 points out of a possible 400.

He finished fifth in the Formula Three Euroseries the following year. Lewis Hamilton and ASM swept the championship; Vettel's ASL team, although being the top rookie, failed to win a single race.

Vettel made his F1 testing debut for the Williams team thanks to his ties at BMW. He had to request a leave of absence from his teacher because he was just 18 years old.

The next year, Vettel joined Paul di Resta at ASM but lost the championship to his teammate. Renault's first World Series appearance was far more successful, as Vettel won both races in Misano.

He again participated in the next race at Spa, but a 170 mph crash severely wounded his hand. His right index finger had to be sewn back together after almost being severed.

BMW

Nevertheless, Vettel became the Friday driver for BMW's F1 team after Robert Kubica was elevated to the race team to replace Jacques Villeneuve.

In Friday practice at his first Grand Prix weekend in Turkey, Vettel was the fastest of all the drivers. He also received a fine for speeding in the pit lane on his way to the track, making him the youngest driver to compete in a Grand Prix weekend at the age of 19 years and 53 days.

2007

He raced in the World Series by Renault to start the 2007 season. Vettel, however, filled in for Kubica at Indianapolis after the Canadian Grand Prix had an injury, finished eighth, becoming the youngest driver to earn a championship point.

Kubica made a comeback at the next race, but Vettel was given another opportunity in Formula 1 later that year.

TORO ROSSO

After the European Grand Prix, Scott Speed was released by Toro Rosso, and Vettel replaced him for the remainder of the campaign.

Vettel collided with the driver in front of him during a safety car period while running a strong third in the wet Japanese Grand Prix. Worse yet, it was fellow Red Bull driver Mark Webber, who had a potential victory in his sights. Vettel turned things around by finishing fourth in the following race in China, which was also held in wet conditions.

2008

Even better the year after, in 2008, when Sebastian Vettel won the wet Italian Grand Prix after winning the pole position and nearly the whole race. He afterwards stated:

I was startled by you during the actual race; you just took the checkered flag in first place, signaling the end of the contest and your maiden Grand Prix victory.

Finally, my extremely reserved engineer called me on the radio to announce that I had won the Italian Grand Prix. I switched on the radio and began speaking calmly and carefully while expressing my gratitude to everyone.

It's ridiculous because you wait your entire life for something similar to happen, and when it does, you have no idea where you are. However, by the time the slow-motion lap was over, it had clicked. I then turned on the radio once more and yelled my appreciation, this time in Italian.

It was the result of the team's season-long rapid advancement. Early in the year, Vettel had trouble progressing past the first lap, but the introduction of the STR3 chassis at Monte-Carlo, followed by an engine improvement, put the team among the front-runners.

RED BULL

2009

By that time, it was already known that Vettel would take over for David Coulthard at Red Bull in 2009. But things didn't go well for him to start his second full F1 season.

He overstepped the line while running in second place at Melbourne, and Kubica crashed into him as a result. Vettel received a grid penalty from the official for the following race in Malaysia, where he also finished last.

This setback came at the start of a year in which he finished second in the drivers' championship. He was successful four times, including his first victory at Monza and a commanding wet-weather triumph in Shanghai.

Vettel scored victories at Silverstone, Suzuka, and Abu Dhabi later in the season when the RB5 was frequently the car to beat. His pursuit of the title was, however, plagued by several missed opportunities, including crashes at Monaco, the Hungaroring, and Istanbul, as well as collisions with Kimi Raikkonen and a mistake on the opening lap while leading. His chances were further hampered by a blown engine at Valencia (his second that weekend).

2010

Vettel ought to have won the first two races of the year, but Red Bull continued their winning streak in 2010. However, he encountered car issues when in the lead in Bahrain and Australia.

He did manage to win in Malaysia, but his teammate Webber quickly took the lead after a run of victories in the middle of the season. Not only were Vettel's car issues frustrating, but he also made some expensive errors. At Istanbul, he struck Webber, and at Spa-Francorchamps, Jenson Button was struck by him.

Nevertheless, he rarely started a race outside of the front row and did so in ten of the 19 events. He found a good vein of success toward the end of the season, winning in Brazil and Japan and leading until his engine failed in Korea.

Even so, going into the season's conclusion in Abu Dhabi, he was the third-ranked title challenger. But in a remarkable turnaround, Vettel earned his fifth victory of the year while rivals Webber and Alonso struggled, snatching the championship from their grasp.

2011

Vettel renewed his contract with Red Bull till the end of 2014 just before the 2011 season began.

Once more, the RB7 was the best car on the track, and this time, Vettel used it to destroy his competitors. He won 11 races out of 19 starts, setting a new record most pole position wins (15). With four races left, he finished the championship.

Vettel significantly outperformed teammate Webber, who managed just one victory in the decisive race in Brazil while Vettel experienced a rare gearbox issue. As he became the first driver to win back-to-back world championship championships since Fernando Alonso in 2006, only this and a first-lap retirement in Abu Dhabi due to a puncture went wrong for Vettel.

2012

After a season-long struggle with Alonso, Vettel was able to successfully defend his championship once more in 2012.

Red Bull had to wage a rearguard action in the first races because to changes in the technical rules. The season started off well for Vettel with a second place finish in Melbourne and a round four victory.

Vettel fell behind in the title race, and Alonso took the lead, as Red Bull attempted to advance with their RB8. Failure of the alternator cost Valencia a possible victory. Webber had evidently adapted to the new car more rapidly at previous tracks.

He lost points in a race that he had already compromised by receiving a penalty when dueling with Alonso in

Italy due to a second alternator failure. In Germany, he made a similar error with Button.

But during the summer break, Vettel's season started to improve. An effective second-place finish in Belgium was the result of a solid drive.

After Hamilton retired in front of him, he won in Singapore. After that, he won four straight races and never trailed in any of them.

Vettel's winning streak came to an end after he overtook Alonso in the championship standings. He was penalized for a technical infraction in Abu Dhabi, but he impressively overcame it to place third. Alonso was dethroned by Hamilton in America, and he entered the championship's penultimate round leading by 13 points.

This turned out to be just enough following a stressful championship race at Interlagos in which Vettel spun out on lap one and was forced to finish the race in a damaged vehicle. While Alonso could only manage second, he managed to finish in sixth place, which was good enough for him to maintain his championship lead.

2013

Vettel's fourth consecutive victory in 2013 added to his winning streak.

The championship's first rounds hinted at a closely contested season, with Vettel sharing victories with Alonso and Raikkonen. Mercedes had a good start to the season as well, with their drivers frequently preventing Vettel from securing pole position in the first half of the championships.

However, consistent podium results preserved Vettel in first place. He disobeyed his team's directive to stay behind Webber and passed his teammate in the final stint during a contentious victory in Malaysia.

Following the summer break, which also fell in line with a mid-season change in tyre composition that benefited Red Bull, Vettel won six straight races, deciding the title with three races remaining. He continued to triumph until the end of the campaign, breaking the previous mark by winning nine straight grand prixs.

2014

Vettel's championship run and winning streak of races came to an end as a result of a significant change in the technical rules. Red Bull, and especially its engine supplier Renault, were not well-prepared for the changeover to V6 hybrid turbo engines.

Vettel, meanwhile, also had trouble getting the most out of the RB11. When the dominant Mercedes cars were beatable, Vettel's new teammate Daniel Ricciardo did considerably better, and it was he who profited rather than Vettel.

In the championship standings, Vettel dropped to fifth, and his rising resentment drove him to make a significant career move. Red Bull and Vettel parted company at the Japanese Grand Prix, and it was later reported that Vettel would be taking Alonso's place at Ferrari.

FERRARI

2015

With no race victories in 2014, Ferrari had an even less competitive season than Red Bull, but in 2015, the team saw a turnaround. The red cars were in contention for victory far sooner than anticipated after fixing some of the basic flaws of their initial V6 hybrid turbo.

And Vettel was leading the way. After following the Mercedes couple home in Melbourne, he put more pressure on them in Malaysia. Due to the early pit stops made by the silver cars as a result of the Safety Car deployment, Vettel seized the opportunity to take the lead in the race. He then utilized the advantage of his car's performance on softer tyres to win the race unexpectedly.

But that wasn't the start of a championship bid. Vettel could not consistently steal points away from Mercedes because they were simply too powerful. He was, however, by far their closest rival: for the remainder of the season, Vettel easily handled his fellow world champion teammate Kimi Raikkonen, who had previously shown promise in Bahrain and China.

More victories followed in Singapore and Hungary, with the latter coming as a result of the Ferrari once more outperforming the Mercedes on a hot circuit with soft rubber. Despite a shock at Spa, where a tyre exploded and prevented what would have been a podium finish, Vettel even led Nico Rosberg's Mercedes in the standings until the final stages of the race.

In the end, he had to be content with third. But after 2014, his three triumphs and 10 other podium places provided the ideal rebuttal to his critics.

2016

Ferrari's second year was only aptly characterized as disappointing. More than that, as he neared the conclusion of his second losing season in three years, Vettel's mounting annoyance turned into pure anger.

The incident occurred in Mexico, where Vettel lost his cool while battling Max Verstappen and roared in anger after the Red Bull driver refused to give up a position that Vettel had been allocated mistakenly.

When the other Red Bull attacked him, Vettel swerved into Daniel Ricciardo after launching a four-word diatribe at race director Charlie Whiting over the radio. He was not punished for the former, but the latter prevented him from placing on the podium.

This occurred toward the end of a season that had a far more promising beginning. If his crew had taken advantage of the chance to swap out his tires when the race was suspended, Vettel would have won in Australia after leading the first few laps of the season. The Mercedes easily passed them after failing to do that.

He missed another win shot in Canada. He got off to another fast start and took the lead, but Ferrari made a rash pit stop this time during the Virtual Safety Car period. The team's rapid pit stop did not help them capitalize on the deployment's abrupt termination, and Vettel's lead was lost.

His seventh outing of the year finished with him finishing on the podium in Abu Dhabi, although the team had hoped for much more from 2016.

2017

Ferrari made a wise choice by concentrating its 2016 development program on the 2017 season, which saw the implementation of new aerodynamic regulations. Vettel led the championship in the first half of the year, and the team got off to a solid start.

Despite a contentious encounter with Hamilton in Azerbaijan, this was the case. Vettel swerved into Hamilton's side, making contact, thinking Hamilton had brake-tested him behind the Safety Car. He was fortunate to finish the race ahead of Hamilton, who had to pit due to a loose headrest, and to only receive a stop-go penalty.

However, Vettel's chances of winning the championship were dashed in the last run of flyaway races. In Singapore, he won the pole position, but his action caused a three-car accident that destroyed both Ferraris as well as Max Verstappen's Red Bull. Hamilton's victory left him in position to win the championship, but Vettel's technical difficulties in Japan all but ended his chances.

Vettel won the championship in Brazil, but Hamilton ultimately secured it in Mexico. Even though the championship escaped him, Ferrari were once again developing championship contenders.

2018

At the start of 2018, there were encouraging signs. Vettel began the season with back-to-back victories in Australia and Bahrain, showing that Ferrari had significantly reduced the horsepower gap to Mercedes.

After easily defeating Mercedes in Canada, it appeared that Vettel was finally on track to win the fifth championship he had been vying for for the previous five years. But it never happened, largely as a result of his mistakes.

In France, he collided with Bottas, had a grid penalty in Austria, and worst of all, he had his SF71H disqualified while leading on his home track. And it didn't stop there.

He lost points for colliding with Hamilton on the opening lap of the race at Monza after taking the lead from Hamilton at Spa. He followed suit with Verstappen in Japan and Ricciardo in Austin, starting a trend. That effectively ended his chances of winning the championship, and Hamilton duly completed the task in Mexico.

2019

Over the following two seasons, Sebastian Vettel's struggles persisted; he only managed one event win in 2019 and no victories in 2020. He and Ferrari split up at the conclusion of the 2020 campaign. He joined Aston Martin in 2021, taking the place of Mexican racer Sergio Pérez.

AWARDS & ACHIEVEMENTS

At the annual Autosport Awards in 2008, Sebastian Vettel won the Rookie of the Year honor.

For his accomplishments in 2008, he received the Lorenzo Bandini Trophy in 2009. He received the German Sports personality of the Year award the following year.

From 2010 to 2013, he won the International Racing Driver category at the Autosport Awards four times in a row.

For being Double successive F1 World Champion at the age of

twenty-four - winner of eleven Grands Prix out of nineteen, he received the Grands Prix de l'Academie des Sports 201, in 2012.

At the age of 24, he won two consecutive F1 World Championships and eleven of the nineteen Grands Prix.

He received the Silberne Lorbeerblatt-Silver Laurel Leaf, Germany's top sporting accolade, that same year in recognition of his several world championship wins.

In 2009 and 2013, he received the F1 driver of the year award. He was the 2009, 2012, and 2013 DHL Fastest Lap Award winner.

In 2012 and 2013, Pap named him the European Sportsperson of the

Year. He received the Laureus World Sports Award's Sportsman of the Year honor in 2014.

PERSONAL LIFE

Switzerland's Thurgovia is where Sebastian Vettel resides. He enjoys British comedies like "Little Britain" and "Monty Python's Life of Brian," and he is a fan of The Beatles.

He was dating Hanna Prater, a buddy from his youth. The couple wed in a secret ceremony in 2019. Together, they are parents to three kids.

It is reported that Sebastian Vettel earns close to $41 million annually.

Chapter two

REASONS FOR SABASTIAN RETIREMENT REVEILED

Sebastian Vettel, a four-time Formula 1 world champion, has declared his retirement at the conclusion of this campaign. The 35-year-old acknowledged that he was **scared** about what the future might hold for him and that his worries about the climate emergency and F1's contribution to the issue played a factor in his decision-making process.

Vettel made his Formula 1 debut in 2007 and is currently an Aston Martin driver. At 23 years and 134 days old, when he won his first championship, he was the sport's youngest world champion. He now has 53 victories.

Between 2010 and 2013, he won four in a row for Red Bull.

Vettel has become more vocal in recent years about social and environmental issues. He recently stated his reluctance about taking part in F1, a sport with a significant carbon footprint due to the amount of plane travel required.

He stated that a number of considerations, including his desire to spend more time with his family and see his three children grow up, as well as his interest in other matters outside of F1, which had come to be of greater significance to him, had led to his decision. Before this weekend's Hungarian Grand Prix, he remarked in Budapest, "I know how difficult this job is, how much effort goes into this, and if you do this, I am confident you have to do it the right way." In addition, take physical time away from your family, children, and home. Additionally, I have developed new hobbies and viewpoints, and I can't ignore these voices. He has already spoken out on environmental problems and especially mentioned the climate emergency as a consideration in his decision-making.

Obviously, he added, "seeing the world, racing automobiles, and actually consuming resources are things that I cannot turn away from." I don't think you can really unsee it once you see these things and are aware of it. There is no way that F1 or any other sport or industry can escape the climate catastrophe because it affects us all. It may be delayed or be more discreet, but all it takes is time, which we don't have.

Printed in Great Britain
by Amazon